YOU CHOOSE™
BOOKS
Historical Eras

THE GREAT DEPRESSION

An Interactive History Adventure

by Michael Burgan

Consultant:
Margaret Rung, Associate Professor of History
Director, Center for New Deal Studies
Roosevelt University
Chicago, Illinois

CAPSTONE PRESS
a capstone imprint

You Choose Books are published by Capstone Press,
151 Good Counsel Drive, P.O. Box 669, Mankato, Minnesota 56002.
www.capstonepub.com
Copyright © 2011 by Capstone Press, a Capstone imprint.
All rights reserved. No part of this publication may be reproduced in whole or in part,
or stored in a retrieval system, or transmitted in any form or by any means, electronic,
mechanical, photocopying, recording, or otherwise, without written permission of the publisher.
For information regarding permission, write to Capstone Press, 151 Good Counsel Drive,
P.O. Box 669, Dept. R, Mankato, Minnesota 56002.

Library of Congress Cataloging-in-Publication Data
Burgan, Michael.
 The Great Depression : an interactive history adventure / by Michael Burgan.
    p. cm. — (You choose: historical eras)
 Includes bibliographical references and index.
    ISBN 978-1-4296-5480-7 (library binding) — ISBN 978-1-4296-6276-5 (paperback)
 1. United States—History—1933-1945—Juvenile literature. 2. United States—
History—1919-1933—Juvenile literature. 3. Depressions—1929—United States—Juvenile
literature. 4. New Deal, 1933-1939—Juvenile literature. 5. United States—Economic
conditions—1918-1945—Juvenile literature. I. Title.
    E806.B9153 2011
    973.91—dc22   2010035041

Editorial Credits
Angie Kaelberer, editor; Bobbie Nuytten, designer; Wanda Winch, media researcher;
    Eric Manske, production specialist

Photo Credits
Corbis: Bettmann, 6, 81, 83, 85, 103; Getty Images: NY Daily News Archive/John Schutz, 44,
NY Daily News Archive/Joseph Costa, 31, Popperfoto, 60, Time Life Pictures/Herbert Gehr,
92; Library of Congress, Prints and Photographs Division, cover, 12, 16, 20, 46, 52, 57, 65, 72,
97, 100, 105; MacArthur Memorial Foundation, 29, 33, 40

Printed in the United States of America in Stevens Point, Wisconsin.
092010   005934WZS11

TABLE OF CONTENTS

ABOUT YOUR ADVENTURE

YOU are living through the Great Depression—the worst economic crisis in U.S. history. The era began in October 1929, as the value of the stock in many large American companies began to fall. Millions of people lost their jobs.

In this book you'll explore how the choices people made meant the difference between life and death. The events you'll experience happened to real people.

Chapter One sets the scene. Then you choose which path to read. Follow the directions at the bottom of each page. The choices you make will change your outcome. After you finish your path, go back and read the others for new perspectives and more adventures.

YOU CHOOSE the path
you take through history.

The stock market's rise in October 1929 led to a huge crash.

CHAPTER 1

From Good Times to Bad

For many Americans the 1920s were the "Roaring Twenties." World War I (1914–1918) was over, and businesses were booming. Many people bought their new goods on credit. They paid a small amount each month, plus interest.

Credit is a form of borrowing. Americans also borrowed to buy stock in companies. As a company sells more stock, the stock's value rises. During the 1920s many people entered the stock market. They believed it would keep rising and that they would make a fortune. A few people did become wealthy. But the gap between the earnings of the richest and poorest Americans was huge.

7

Turn the page.

Unemployment rate 1929–1939
☐ 15%–25%
▨ More than 25%

Farmers didn't share in the great wealth of the 1920s. Many had loans to pay, so they produced more crops and livestock. But people weren't buying more food than they had before, and the price of farm products fell.

Many farmers lost their farms. Poor farming practices and drought also created a desert in a large area of the Midwest. People called it the Dust Bowl.

In 1929 a crisis hit Wall Street in New York City. Most buying and selling of U.S. stocks took place there. Companies that had loaned money to stock investors began to ask for their money back. Investors didn't have the cash, so they sold their stocks to raise it. As they sold, the value of the stocks fell. October 24, 1929, was called Black Thursday, as stock prices plunged. They fell even more on October 29—Black Tuesday.

By this time many companies were having trouble getting loans. They began to fire workers. As a result people bought fewer products. Each year hundreds of banks went out of business, wiping out their customers' savings.

Turn the page.

World War I veterans were among those hardest hit. Many soldiers gave up well-paying jobs to serve in the armed forces. Congress agreed to give these men a bonus to make up for their lost wages, payable in 1945. But that wouldn't help the veterans during the Depression. Many of them came to Washington, D.C., to protest. They were called the Bonus Army.

President Herbert Hoover hoped charities and state and local governments could help people. But those groups didn't have enough money to help everyone.

In 1932 Hoover ran again for president. His opponent was Franklin D. Roosevelt. FDR, as he was called, won the election. He promised a "new deal" for Americans. That phrase became the name for the government programs he proposed.

One of the largest New Deal programs was the Works Progress Administration. Starting in 1935 the WPA put people to work building roads, public buildings, and parks. Others took photos, painted murals on buildings, or wrote plays and books. The WPA soon became the nation's largest employer. Another program, the Civilian Conservation Corps, provided jobs for thousands of young men.

You are facing hard times. Will the New Deal help you? Is there anything you can do to help yourself?

11

➤ To be a former soldier seeking government help, turn to page 13.

➤ To be a teenager living the life of a hobo, turn to page 47.

➤ To be a young man working for the Civilian Conservation Corps, turn to page 73.

World War I veterans protested in Washington, D.C., in July 1932.

CHAPTER 2

MARCHING TO WASHINGTON

It's June 17, 1932. Rising ahead of you is the dome of the U.S. Capitol. It's been a long trip from your home in Ohio to Washington, D.C. Your back aches from the freight train ride. You don't have a car and couldn't afford to buy a ticket on a passenger train.

Walking nearby or riding in trucks are men just like you—veterans of the world war. When the United States entered the war in 1917, you were glad to serve. You came home in late 1918 to parades honoring your bravery.

13

Turn the page.

Now you and other vets are part of another parade. You call yourselves the Bonus Expeditionary Force. The newspapers call you the Bonus Army or Bonus Marchers. A veteran named Walter Waters is your leader.

You're marching to Washington to get what you think you deserve. When you joined the army, you gave up a good job in a factory. Your military pay was much lower.

In 1924 the U.S. government said it would give each veteran a certificate that would mature and be paid in 1945. This money would make up for what you lost during the war. Soldiers who served stateside would receive $1 per day served. Those who served overseas would get $1.25 for each day of service. With the interest that would build up on the certificates, each soldier would receive about $1,000.

Waiting more than 20 years to get your service bonus was fine with you at first. But then the Great Depression came. You lost your job. Your friend Bill lost his as well. You remember what he said before you both left for Washington. "We can't wait until 1945 to get that money. We need it now!"

There is one way a veteran's family can get the money before 1945—if he dies. The veterans call that money the tombstone bonus. Your wife died two years ago, and you don't have any children, but you still need the money to live.

You come to an area of Washington called Anacostia Flats. Up ahead a group of men is outside a camp filled with tents and shanties. One says, "I hear some fellows are camped downtown. I'm going there."

Turn the page.

"This camp looks all right," Bill says. "Why not stay here?"

The Anacostia Flats camp was filled with makeshift tents.

→ To stay, go to page **17**.

→ To go to the other camp, turn to page **28**.

You walk into the camp. The muddy ground is dotted with tents. Some are made from old clothes and other cloth.

"Hello there," a man calls out. His wife and two children stand by his side. They're next to a real tent, like the ones soldiers use in the field. "I'm Arnie Smith, and this is my wife, Helen."

"Hello," you say. "Any chance we can get a tent like that?"

Arnie shakes his head. "Doubt it. The police didn't give us many. The chief, Pelham Glassford, is trying to help us when he can. But nobody expected this many folks to come here."

"They say there's at least 15,000," Helen adds. "And more coming every day, from all over the country."

Turn the page.

"So where are we going to sleep?" Bill asks you. You see men carrying old metal frames and boxes. They're coming from a dump just outside the camp.

"Let's check out the dump and see what we can find," you say.

"You're welcome to camp here," Arnie says.

A black man comes up the path carrying some clothes. He nods to you and says hello to the Smiths. He begins to hang the wet clothes on a tree. Bill looks at the man and shakes his head. "Let's go to another part of the camp," he says.

"But this seems fine," you tell him, puzzled.

"Stay if you want," Bill says, "but I'm going."

→ To stay with the Smiths, go to page **19**.

→ To go with Bill, turn to page **24**.

"I'm staying," you tell your friend. Bill gives the black man a dirty look as he walks away.

"Your friend doesn't like people like me?" the man asks. "Black people?"

"I'm sorry," you say, embarrassed.

"Doesn't matter," the man says. He offers you his hand. "My name's Ed. Yeah, I see plenty of that outside. But there's no racism here in Camp Marks. Everybody suffers the same, black or white. Everybody wants the same thing—food and a job. Too bad more folks can't see us getting along so well."

Ed offers to let you share his tent, and you gladly agree.

"What do you think of our camp?" Ed asks.

"Never saw anything like it," you reply.

19

Turn the page.

"We've got a barbershop," Ed says, "and there's talk we'll have our own newspapers soon. Musicians give concerts, and the guys play baseball. Parents give their kids school lessons. And we've got our own guards to keep order."

Some Bonus Marchers brought their families with them.

You begin to unpack the few items you brought. A man runs down the muddy path outside the tent.

"Commander Waters needs volunteers!" the man shouts. "We're going to the Capitol!"

"What's going on at the Capitol?" you ask Ed.

"Big vote today in Congress. The House of Representatives has already said it would give us our bonus money now. The Senate votes today. If we win that, we're one step closer. But President Hoover still has to sign the bill."

"Will he?" you ask.

"He might if a few thousand vets come down to the Capitol today. I'm going. What about you?"

➤ To stay at the camp, turn to page 22.

➤ To go to the Capitol, turn to page 35.

"I just got here," you tell Ed. "I'd better get settled in first."

Late that afternoon thousands of men try to leave for the Capitol. When they reach the 11th Street drawbridge over the Potomac River, they find that police have raised it. Other bridges are closed as well. After complaints from Washington citizens, though, the police open the bridge. Veterans start pouring onto the Capitol grounds.

You're sleeping in Ed's tent when he comes in and wakes you. "Bad news," he says. "The Senate voted against the bill."

Commander Waters sends the message that he will stay until 1945, if that's what it takes to get the money. But in the weeks that follow, food supplies dwindle. Many people pack up their belongings. The Smiths are among them.

"Did you hear about the government money?" Helen asks you. "They'll pay us a little to help us get home, but we have to leave by July 15."

"I heard," you say, "but I haven't got anywhere to go. No family, no job, no place to stay."

"You're welcome to travel with us," Arnie says. It's a generous offer. But there's still a chance the bonus money could come through.

➤ To go with the Smiths, turn to page 37.

➤ To stay at the camp, turn to page 38.

You realize Bill wanted to leave because of the black man. You didn't know Bill was prejudiced toward black people. But he's your only friend here, so you keep quiet. As you walk you notice that blacks and whites are living side by side in the camp. Maybe being in the Bonus Army will change Bill's ideas.

"What about there?" Bill says. He points to a spot at the edge of the camp. You nod, then head to the dump while Bill holds the spot. Along the way you see a small group of people around a man standing on a wooden box.

"This Depression is a sign, friends," the speaker says. "Capitalism is doomed. We need new ideas."

"Are you talking about Communism?" someone calls out. "About taking away people's property and giving it to the government?"

"I thought Commies weren't allowed in the camps," a man says to the speaker. The man looks around. "Come on, let's get this guy!" Others in the crowd rush toward the speaker.

"Fellas, please …" the frightened speaker stammers as he backs away.

"I'll bet you aren't even a vet!" the leader of the crowd shouts at him. Then he looks at you.

"Are you gonna help us? Or are you a Commie too?"

→ To join the crowd, turn to page **26**.

→ To refuse, turn to page **41**.

You join the crowd, which is now chasing the man through the mud. As the speaker darts between the tents and shacks, he slips. The crowd circles around him. With about 15 men against one, this wouldn't be a fair fight.

"Hold on," you say. The men turn and look at you. "I hate this Commie talk. But we shouldn't beat up this guy. Let's call the police. We still believe in law and order, don't we?"

A few men grumble, but most nod their heads. "All right," the leader says. "We'll call the police. But if he ever sets foot in this camp again …"

Other voices cry out: "Yeah!" "Right!" "We'll get him!"

"Thanks," the speaker says to you.

"You Communists are making us Bonus Marchers look bad," you say. "But no one should get beat up for speaking his mind."

You hadn't realized this place could be so dangerous. You walk back to your spot, where Bill is still waiting. He's talking to another man. You tell both of them what happened.

"This camp can be kind of rough," the other man says. "I'm moving downtown. You two should come with me."

Turn the page.

You look at Bill. "Maybe it would be better there," you tell him.

"You go ahead," he says. "I'm staying here."

You say good-bye to Bill and walk away with the other man. "My name's John," the man says. "From Kentucky."

The two of you walk to lower Pennsylvania Avenue. Just up the street, President Herbert Hoover lives in the White House.

You and John end up in a partly torn-down building. The government has let the vets live in a few of these buildings. The vets named the area Camp Glassford, in honor of Washington Police Chief Pelham Glassford. He has tried to help the marchers. Tents and lean-tos surround the crumbling buildings.

As the days go by, you hear bad news. Congress has refused to pass a bill that will give you your bonus now. The leader of the Bonus Army, Walter Waters, says he will stay in Washington until 1945 if he has to.

John says, "The newspaper says the government will pay for us to take a train home. I might do it. What about you?"

Camp Glassford was made up of gutted downtown buildings.

→ To stay in Washington, turn to page **30**.

→ To go home, turn to page **45**.

You tell John, "If enough of us stay, maybe the lawmakers will change their minds."

John shakes his head. "Maybe. Well, good luck to you. I'm leaving."

The government set a deadline of July 15 for all the vets to leave. But when that day comes, you and several thousand other vets are still at Camp Glassford, along with some wives and children. Another week passes. Rumors spread that Commander Waters is trying to work out a deal with the government. You also hear that army troops are preparing to force you out.

On the morning of July 28, you walk over to Pennsylvania Avenue to hear Commander Waters speak. He says the government is going to move you all out of the camp to a new one on private land outside the city.

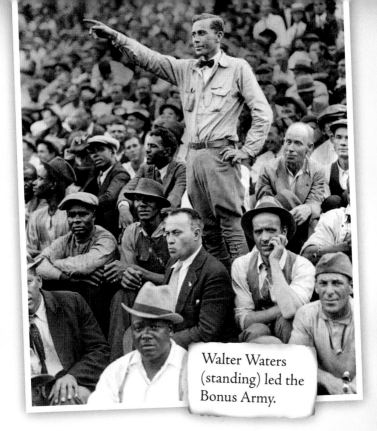

Walter Waters (standing) led the Bonus Army.

"We can't lick the United States government, but when the United States troops are called to escort me out, I'm going out," he says.

Some men around you grumble as they walk back to their shelters. They're still not ready to leave.

➤ To wait for the evacuation, turn to page 32.

➤ To leave now, turn to page 45.

At 10:00 a.m. the police show up at Camp Glassford. They go first to the old National Guard armory to escort people out. Most leave peacefully. You're watching the evacuation when a group of veterans breaks through a roped-off area. As the police rush to stop them, someone tears Chief Glassford's badge off his chest. Some vets start throwing bricks and rocks at the police officers.

"Duck!" someone shouts just as a brick sails past your head and hits an officer. Chief Glassford runs into the center of the fight and calms things down. Several police officers and veterans are hurt, but not seriously.

As the day goes on, the men at the Anacostia Flats camp hear about the evacuation. Thousands of them stream into the city. To your surprise, you bump into your friend Bill.

On July 28, 1932, a
planned evacuation
turned violent.

The two of you are standing near a vacant

office building when a fight breaks out. Glassford

and several officers run up the building's outside

stairway. Men on the second floor throw bricks

and a garbage can at the officers.

Turn the page.

One officer pulls out his gun. He points it in your direction! As two shots ring through the air, you grab Bill's arm, pulling him along as you fall to the ground.

"Help! I've been shot!" one vet screams just a few feet away from you. Another vet lies lifeless on the ground. Glassford yells at his officers to put their guns away.

Three officers have also been wounded. After an ambulance takes the dead and wounded away, the crowd quiets down.

➤ To stay, turn to page 43.

➤ To leave now, turn to page 45.

You and Ed join hundreds of men walking into the center of Washington. Several thousand are gathered around the steps and on the lawn of the Capitol.

About 9:30 p.m., Commander Waters appears. He tells you the Senate voted against the bill. All around you, thousands of men fall silent. But some are angry. They could erupt in violence any minute. A woman next to Waters whispers to him. He turns and shouts for everyone to sing "America the Beautiful." You all sing and then go peacefully back to your camps.

But the battle isn't over. Waters soon calls for recruits to find more veterans to come to Washington. He promises to stay until 1945, if needed, to get that bonus money. You talk about the future with Ed.

Turn the page.

"I've stayed here long enough," he says. "I'm going back to Tennessee."

"I've got nothing to go back to in Ohio," you say. "I'm going to try to get more veterans to come here." You see a truck pulling out of the camp. Its box is filled with men. On its side is written, "Back to Washington with Recruits."

You don't know where the truck is going, but it doesn't matter. You run to the truck with your arms outstretched. Two men in the box pull you aboard. You're going to keep trying to get your fellow veterans the money they deserve.

THE END

To follow another path, turn to page 11.
To read the conclusion, turn to page 101.

You smile at him. "Arnie, that's a kind offer. The best one I've had since this Depression started. I'd be glad to travel with your family."

Ed is returning to his home in Tennessee. You tell him good-bye before you roll up your few belongings and take one last look around the camp. You squeeze into the Smiths' ancient Ford. You're heading for California. Arnie heard there are jobs there in the fields and orchards. Even if that isn't true, it's got to be better than waiting here for something that probably will never come.

THE END

To follow another path, turn to page 11.
To read the conclusion, turn to page 101.

The summer drags on. You're thin from the lack of food and tired of bathing in the Anacostia River and sleeping on the muddy ground. Late in July you run into Bill. "Commander Waters says the army will force us out if we don't go quietly," he tells you.

You don't believe that will happen. But on July 28, you read in the newspaper that the U.S. Army is marching today. They're forcing out vets camped in old buildings downtown.

"Think they'll come here?" Bill asks you.

"It's the biggest camp," you reply. "They won't let us stay."

Sure enough, shortly after sunset you see the troops marching over the bridge that connects Anacostia Flats to the city. Some soldiers ride horses. A few steer tanks across the bridge. Most travel on foot, their rifles on their backs.

"Everybody out!" a soldier yells. You've heard that several vets were killed in the city earlier in the day. You know the soldiers mean business. You quickly roll up everything you own. A few people boo the soldiers. A soldier then throws something into the crowd. A cloud of tear gas spreads.

As you run from the cloud of choking gas, soldiers set the shacks on fire. Some veterans light fires as well. The flames shoot high into the dark sky.

A tall, straight figure is barking orders. His face looks familiar. You're shocked to realize that he's General Douglas MacArthur, the U.S. Army chief of staff. If MacArthur is against the Bonus Marchers, you know that the situation is hopeless.

Turn the page.

You keep running until you reach a street of neighborhood shops. You settle in a grocery store doorway to catch a few hours' sleep. You'll start the long trip back to Ohio in the morning.

Soldiers used tear gas to force the marchers from the camps.

THE END

To follow another path, turn to page 11.
To read the conclusion, turn to page 101.

"I don't believe in Communism," you say, "but a man's got a right to speak his mind."

"Let him do it outside the camp," the leader of the group says. "If the government people think we're Commies, we'll never get our bonuses."

Meanwhile, the speaker is trying to slip away. The men run after him. They catch him at the edge of the camp. You run over and try to pull some of the men off the speaker.

"What's the big idea?" one man says. He throws a punch at your jaw. Another fist crashes into the side of your head. You go down. Next to you is the speaker. His nose is bloody as he tries to defend himself from worn boots kicking his body.

Turn the page.

A voice suddenly rises above the sounds of the fight. "All right, all right, break it up." It's a camp police officer. The men around you drop their fists to their sides.

"We found a Commie," one man says. "And this one," he says, pointing at you, "was trying to help him."

"I'm no Commie!" you insist, your jaw aching.

The camp officer looks you over. "Well, we've called in the Washington police. You can tell your story to the judge."

You've been arrested for helping a man! At least in jail you'll get food and a place to sleep away from the mud.

THE END

To follow another path, turn to page 11.
To read the conclusion, turn to page 101.

The streets are quiet for a bit. Later in the afternoon you hear new sounds. The clop of horses on the street, the roar of tank engines, and the steady marching steps of soldiers. The U.S. Army has arrived!

The soldiers begin pushing you out of the area. Some men resist, and a few soldiers throw grenades. After several explosions, tear gas fills the street. Your eyes begin to water and burn. Meanwhile, the soldiers set fire to the tents and shacks around the buildings. A few vets fight back, heaving bricks at the soldiers on horseback. You keep moving, trying to escape the growing clouds of gas.

In less than 30 minutes, the battle is over. The vets and their families flee as smoke from burning tents and shanties fills the air.

Turn the page.

Bill finds you in the crowd. "Two more veterans were killed," he gasps. "It's time to leave. I hear that the mayor of Johnstown, Pennsylvania, is offering to take in us vets."

"What are we waiting for?" you ask him. "Let's go!" You're still poor and homeless, but at least you are alive.

Veterans camped near Johnstown, Pennsylvania, for a few weeks.

THE END

To follow another path, turn to page 11.
To read the conclusion, turn to page 101.

You already have your things with you, so you head down toward the train station. You can go home, but there's nothing waiting for you there. Maybe it's better to be a hobo. You can ride the trains across the country, seeking work wherever you go. But whatever happens, you're glad you joined the Bonus Army to fight for what you deserve.

THE END

To follow another path, turn to page 11.
To read the conclusion, turn to page 101.

Franklin D. Roosevelt (center) took office on March 4, 1933.

CHAPTER 3

RIDING THE RAILS

"I'm so hungry," your brother Bobby says. "When's Mama going to find another job?"

It's June 1933, and a month has passed since Mama lost her job at the shoe factory. Your father went to California late last year, trying to find work. He hasn't written in weeks. The kitchen cabinets are almost bare. Your two little sisters, Jane and Molly, cry every night because they go to bed hungry.

"President Roosevelt says he's going to create jobs," you say. "But who knows when Mama will get one—if she can get one."

Bobby stands. "Mr. Roosevelt also said we've got nothing to fear but fear itself. We can't be afraid. We've got to do something."

Turn the page.

"Like what?" you ask.

"Get jobs to help Mama. After all, I'm 14 and you're 15. We're old enough to work."

"You know there are no jobs in this part of Indiana," you reply impatiently.

"Then we can ride the rails. Take the trains to where the work is. I've read about kids our age doing that."

"Bobby, maybe a boy like you can do it. But I'm a girl. Besides, it's dangerous."

48

"Maybe," Bobby says. "But we have to do something." He's already stuffing his few clothes in a pillowcase. "Are you coming?"

➻ To stay home, go to page 49.

➻ To go with Bobby, turn to page 53.

"Go if you have to," you say. "Just be careful! And write to us when you find a place to stay."

Bobby goes out the back door and heads toward the railroad station. An hour later your mother comes home, Molly and Jane tagging behind her. She's carrying a loaf of bread and some apples.

"The church didn't have much to give today," she says. "Where's Bobby?"

"Not sure," you lie. "Probably out playing ball."

"With your father gone, Bobby could get into trouble. Since you're the oldest, I hope you'll keep an eye out for him."

"Yes, ma'am." Your stomach churns with worry. How could you have been so stupid? Bobby can't be out there by himself.

To go after Bobby, turn to page **50**.

To tell your mother where Bobby is, turn to page **57**.

You run to the rail yard, hoping to catch Bobby before he leaves. Your heart sinks as you see a train pulling away.

"Looking for someone?" You turn and see a short, bearded man coming over a hill near the train station. His clothes are dusty and worn.

"My brother," you say. "I think he was on that train."

"You wanted to go with him, or you were trying to stop him?"

"Trying to stop him. How many girls go riding the rails?"

"Oh, more than you might think," the man replies.

"Are you a bum?" you ask.

The man's face reddens. "Missy, if you're going to spend any time around the jungles, you better watch your words. A bum just stays in one place looking for handouts. Won't work to save his life. Me, I'm a hobo. I work for my food. When I can find work." He holds out his hand. "They call me Shorty."

You shake his hand. "What did you mean, the 'jungles'?"

He motions you to follow him over the hill. On the other side, you see cardboard shanties and a group of people around a campfire.

Shorty says, "Welcome to our jungle. That's the name for our little camp by the tracks. And not just hoboes here, either. Some families come down too. Anyone's welcome. Just don't cause any trouble, and share whatever food you got."

Turn the page.

Shorty motions to a big pot over the campfire.

"You hungry? Stay and eat."

Hoboes cooked their meals over campfires in the jungles.

→ To stay at the camp, turn to page **59**.

→ To go after Bobby, turn to page **61**.

You race into your room and throw some clothes into a bag. As you head to the rail yard, Bobby tells you what he learned from the boys at school.

"When we get to a town, we can go to houses and ask to work for food. Some people will just give it to you for nothing. And the hoboes leave signs on houses and buildings that will tell you the good places to go."

"What kind of signs?" you ask.

"Well, a drawing of a table means the folks might ask you to come in for a meal. A smiling cat means a kind woman lives there. And an X with a circle around it means they'll probably give you something to take with you."

Turn the page.

As you reach the rail yard, Bobby leads you over a hill behind the tracks. You see cardboard shanties and a group of people around a campfire.

Bobby goes over to one man sitting at the fire. After a minute he comes back. "There's two trains just about ready to leave," Bobby tells you. "One's heading to Chicago, and the other down south."

It would be exciting to go to Chicago. The World's Fair is going on there. But in the south, farms might be looking for workers.

➼ *To go to Chicago, go to page 55.*

➼ *To head south, turn to page 71.*

"Let's go to Chicago. I want to see the World's Fair," you say.

Bobby leads you to the track. "Careful," he says. "Don't let a bull see you. That's what hoboes call the rail yard police. Bulls can have us arrested. Some of them will beat up or even kill a hobo if they find one."

You look around. No one's in sight. You follow Bobby as he climbs into an empty freight car. After a few stops, your stomach is grumbling. You haven't eaten since breakfast, and it's almost dark.

"Maybe we should get off soon and look for some food," you say.

"I'm hungry too. But if we get off, who knows when we can catch another train heading our way."

To keep riding, turn to page **56**.

To get off at the next station, turn to page **64**.

"You're right," you say. "Let's keep going until morning. It'll be easier to look for food then anyway."

You and Bobby fall asleep on the hard floor of the railroad car. You awake hours later. A group of teenage boys joined you during the night. You feel the train come to a stop.

"Where are we?" you ask.

"Chicago," one of the boys says. "Almost right downtown."

You wake Bobby. "Come on, let's go to the fair!"

"You need money to get in," he says, still rubbing sleep from his eyes. "We need to get jobs first, don't you think?"

➤ To go to the fair, turn to page **65**.

➤ To look for a job, turn to page **68**.

About 250,000 young people became hoboes during the Depression.

You run into the kitchen. "Mama, I do know where Bobby is. He went down to the rail yard to catch a ride."

"Why did you let him go?" Mama demands.

"Because we need food! And he wanted to do something. You think he's the only teenager out looking for work to help his family?"

Turn the page.

Mama picks up the phone and calls the police. From what she says, it sounds as if the officer knows all about Bobby. She hangs up and smiles.

"They caught him before he could get into a railcar. They're bringing him home."

You are sorry that you had to tell on Bobby. And your family still needs help. You decide to look for a job tomorrow. Maybe someone would want you to do housecleaning or babysit. Even if they only paid you in food, it would be enough to help your family.

THE END

To follow another path, turn to page 11.
To read the conclusion, turn to page 101.

"Well, a little food would be good," you say. Shorty leads you to the fire. The hoboes are tossing carrots, potatoes, and other vegetables into the pot.

"We call that Mulligan stew," Shorty explains. "Whatever you've found during the day goes into the pot at night. We go down the main streets, looking for scraps of food. Hitting the stems, we call it. Some of what we find is pretty bad. But today we got lots of good stuff, even some meat."

When the stew's ready, you sit around the fire. Everyone talks about all the places they've been. You could listen to their tales forever. But then you remember Bobby. And your mother! She must be worried sick.

"Shorty, I have to go. But I'll be back. And I'll bring something for the stew."

Turn the page.

You're still worried about Bobby and what's going to happen to him. You only hope that he'll meet someone as nice as Shorty to help him along the way.

Hopping on a moving train could lead to injury or death.

THE END

To follow another path, turn to page 11.
To read the conclusion, turn to page 101.

"I really have to find my brother," you tell Shorty.

"All right," he says. "There should be a train heading that way real soon. But it's not safe for a girl alone on the rails. We've got to make you look like a boy." Shorty goes around the camp, asking the hoboes if they can spare some clothes. He comes back with a man's jacket.

"Put this on," he says. Then he hands you a cap. "And put your hair up under this."

You do as he says. Shorty nods. "It will do. Just remember to try to talk a little lower, like a boy. And take this." He hands you a small knife. "Tuck this in your shoe. If anybody bothers you, wave it around."

Turn the page.

You hear two toots of a train whistle. "That signal means the train's just about to go," Shorty says. "Come on!"

You follow him as he runs down to the track. The train is already rolling. You see an open door in a boxcar.

"Run alongside," Shorty yells, "and grab the railing while you put your foot on the stirrup. Then pull yourself up."

Your heart pounds as you run alongside the moving train. You do just as Shorty tells you and pull yourself into the boxcar. It's empty except for two hoboes lying on the floor.

"Where you going?" one of the men asks. You try to sound like a boy as you explain about Bobby and meeting Shorty.

"I know Shorty," the other hobo says. "He's a good guy. We'll help you track down your brother. We know lots of folks along this route."

You heave a sigh of relief. You hope you can find Bobby and bring him home before Mama gets too worried. But if not, maybe you'll have your own adventures riding the rails.

THE END

To follow another path, turn to page 11.
To read the conclusion, turn to page 101.

Soon the train rolls to a stop. You and Bobby step out of the car. Up ahead you see a man standing against another boxcar.

"Hey, you kids!" the man calls.

"A bull!" Bobby says. "Run!" He begins to run down one of the tracks. You follow him. Glancing behind, you see the bull running after you. You fall sideways, landing outside the track.

"Run, Bobby!" you scream, as the bull grabs your arm. But Bobby turns back to help you. The man grabs him as well.

"Come on, kids," the bull says gruffly. "I have to take you down to jail for the night."

At least you'll have a warm place to sleep. You'll figure out where you're going to next in the morning.

THE END

To follow another path, turn to page 11.
To read the conclusion, turn to page 101.

"Maybe we can sneak in," you say. "Come on!"

You see signs for the fair. It's just a few blocks away. But guards are all around.

Most riders were boys, but some girls joined them on the trains.

Turn the page.

"Look," Bobby says, pointing at a guard sleeping near a storage area. As you reach the guard, you sprint past. You're inside!

"This must have cost millions of dollars," Bobby says as he looks around the fairgrounds. You nod, thinking how many poor people could use that money. But even in the Great Depression, people need to have fun. And the fair provides jobs as well. Suddenly you have an idea.

"Bobby, maybe we could get jobs here." You walk over to a food stand. The woman running it looks at you suspiciously. "What can I get you?" she asks.

"Actually, my brother and I are looking for jobs," you tell her.

The woman snorts. "You and everyone else! Don't you know that all the jobs at the fair were filled months ago? Now if you're not going to buy anything, beat it!"

You and Bobby quickly walk away. You spend the rest of the day asking everyone you see about a job. They all give you the same answer. Finally you end up at a hot dog stand just before the fair closes. The owner gives you each a cold hot dog he was about to throw away. You munch on the hot dogs as you walk back to the train station. Maybe you'll have better luck somewhere else.

THE END

To follow another path, turn to page 11.
To read the conclusion, turn to page 101.

You and Bobby walk downtown. You stop at all the stores you see and ask if they need help. The answer is always no.

You keep walking until you come to a street of large, well-kept homes. You see one with grass that needs mowing. That gives you an idea. You run up to the door and ring the doorbell.

An elderly woman answers. "Yes?" she asks.

"Ma'am, I notice that your lawn needs mowing," you say. "My brother and I would be glad to help you for something to eat."

"My regular gardener has been sick," the woman says as she looks at the lawn. "I suppose you can do it. My garden also needs weeding."

You and Bobby spend the next several hours working in the hot sun. Bobby pushes the mower while you pull every weed in the garden.

When you're done, the woman comes out of the house. She nods approvingly at the work you've done. "Come inside for some lemonade and food," she tells you. "My name is Mrs. Ambrose."

You troop into Mrs. Ambrose's kitchen. Inside are two plates heaped with ham sandwiches, potato salad, canned peaches, and big slices of chocolate cake. You both eat until you're full, and then politely thank Mrs. Ambrose as you stand up to leave.

"Wait," she tells you. She reaches into her purse and hands you a dollar. A dollar! That will buy food for a few more days. "I have friends in the neighborhood who might need help with chores as well, if you want to come back tomorrow."

Turn the page.

"Yes, we'll be back," you tell her. As you and Bobby walk down the street, he asks, "Where are we going to sleep tonight?"

"We'll figure something out," you tell him. "At least we've got food and the chance of more work. Maybe we can even save some money to send to Mama." For the first time in months, you feel some hope for the future.

THE END

To follow another path, turn to page 11.
To read the conclusion, turn to page 101.

As you walk toward the southbound train, it slowly begins to pull away. Bobby runs for an open car door and jumps inside. "Come on!" he yells. You take a few strides and put out your arm. Bobby grabs for it, but misses.

You try to run faster alongside the train, but just then, you trip over your shoelace and fall onto the tracks. Bobby's horrified face is the last thing you see as you slip under the wheels of the train.

THE END

To follow another path, turn to page 11.
To read the conclusion, turn to page 101.

The CCC gave young men food, shelter, and job skills.

CHAPTER 4

BUILDING A NATION

Your mother fights back tears as you sign the papers. "You sure you want to do this?" she asks.

"Mom, we need the money," you say. "And it will be good for me to work outdoors."

"The woods are dangerous. What if a bear attacks you? Or what if they put you up on a mountain, and there's a mudslide?"

"As if it's not dangerous living in New York City," you say. "I could be run over by a car anytime I cross the street."

You finish signing your name. At 17, you've dropped out of high school to take this job. You're joining the Civilian Conservation Corps.

73

Turn the page.

President Franklin Roosevelt created the CCC about five years ago, right after he took office in 1933. CCC enrollees are young men, most between 17 and 25. They work outdoors building dams, stopping soil erosion, planting trees, and improving parks. It will be hard work, but you think you're ready for the challenge. And the money you send home will put food on the table. You'll keep just $5 spending money of the $30 you earn each month.

You hand the papers to the clerk, who looks through them. "You're all set. And you're in luck today. We have spots open in two places. You can go upstate here in New York, to Gilbert Lake State Park. Or you can go to Nevada."

⇥ *To go to Gilbert Lake, go to page 75.*
⇥ *To go to Nevada, turn to page 77.*

Your mother will be happier if you stay in the state. A few days later, you report to an army camp in the city for two weeks of basic military training.

A sergeant greets you as you arrive. "I'm Sergeant Willis. Welcome to 'Roosevelt's Tree Army.' Except for not firing a gun, it's a lot like the real army."

Willis explains the schedule you'll follow every workday at Gilbert Lake. A bugle call wakes you at 6:00 a.m., then breakfast at 6:30, and out to work by 7:15. You'll return to the camp at 4:00 p.m. Dinner follows the lowering of the flag. You then have some free time until the lights go out at 10:00 p.m.

Turn the page.

You feel overwhelmed as you head to your barracks. You told Sergeant Willis that you can take the tough schedule, but you're not so sure. When you get to the barracks, you learn that some of the other guys are also unhappy.

"What's it going to be like out in the woods?" a guy named Joey asks the group. "No cars, no movie theaters, no excitement."

"I hear some guys go AWOL—absent without leave," another guy says. "They sneak out of the camp."

"You know what?" Joey asks. "I'm going tonight. Once they send us to Gilbert Lake, we'll be stuck there." He looks at you. "You want to come along?"

→ To stay, turn to page 79.

→ To go AWOL, turn to page 86.

You finish two weeks of basic army training and then head west by train. Joining you are other young men from New York City. Like you, most of them have never left the city before. In Nevada you stop first at a camp in Reno. At the mess hall, you see mounds of food. You fill your plate with steak, potatoes, gravy, and biscuits. You haven't eaten this well in years.

You soon move on to the small town of Hawthorne. Two camps are located there on the grounds of the U.S. Naval Ammunition Depot.

For several weeks you and the other enrollees chop down trees in preparation for a road that will soon be built. You live in a "spike camp" away from the main camp and sleep in tents. The food's not that great, but there's plenty of it. When the weekend comes, you enjoy the chance to rest, read, and write letters home.

Turn the page.

One day the camp commander calls a meeting. "I know most of you like it here in Hawthorne," he says. "But we need some fellows to go over to Arizona. There have been some fires up in the mountains there, and we want to train more firefighters."

Fighting fires could be dangerous. But it could also be exciting.

→ To stay at Hawthorne, turn to page **82**.

→ To go to Arizona, turn to page **84**.

You get through the two weeks of basic training and then board a bus bound for Gilbert Lake. On the bus you meet Dan, a guy a couple of years older than you. He's already done one six-month stay at the state park. Enrollees can sign up four times total, if they need the money.

"I helped build this," Dan says, pointing to the road. Dan describes how the park looked before his first time there. It was mostly wilderness. "But we built the roads and cabins and helped set up a wildlife refuge."

You reach the camp, find your barracks, and settle in your cot for the night. The next morning you see Dan at breakfast.

"I'm starving," you tell him.

"You came to the right place," Dan says. "You'll eat better than you have in years."

Turn the page.

Dan's right. You're amazed to see plenty of bacon, eggs, and pancakes spread out on the tables. You finish your first plate and go back for another two helpings.

Your first day goes by fast. You help build a cabin. You discover you're handy with a hammer. The next day you're assigned to help build a beach by the lakeshore. A middle-aged man approaches you. "You ever work a dump truck before?" he asks.

"No, sir."

"Well, now's a good time to learn."

The man's name is Walter. He's what the CCC calls a local experienced man. The LEMs are older than the enrollees, and they have skills the recruits lack.

Many CCC members helped build roads through forests.

By the weekend, you and Dan are both ready for some fun. "We can stay here and watch a movie," he says, "or we can go into town. The army will drive us over to the local dance."

→ *To stay for the movie, turn to page **88**.*

→ *To go into town, turn to page **90**.*

As some of the enrollees head off for their new assignment, you go with Bert. He's older than most of the guys and served in the world war. Bert is in charge of building a reservoir for the local cattle.

"Grab a shovel and a pick!" Bert orders. "We have a lot to do and not much time to do it."

You dig and pick, forming a pool for the water. You haul large rocks to line the bottom of the reservoir. Sweat pours down your forehead, and your shoulder muscles ache.

"I never worked so hard in my life," you tell your friend Frank Taylor, who's working next to you. He just nods.

At lunchtime you take out the sandwiches and fruit they gave you back at camp. You still have time before you have to go back to work, so Bert says you can go to a nearby pond for a swim.

Over by some rocks, you see something move. You walk over with Frank to take a look. "Looks like a big snake," Frank says.

Living in the city, you've never seen a live snake before. You're curious and want a better look. But what if it's dangerous? Maybe you should tell Bert about it.

Young men from the city had to be taught about snakes and other wildlife.

83

→ To see the snake better, turn to page **93**.

→ To tell Bert, turn to page **95**.

You and the others climb into trucks and head for Arizona. On the ride you talk with Jose, an enrollee from New Mexico. He says he lived near forests like the ones you're headed to. "All it takes is one bolt of lightning to start a pretty mean fire," he says.

You reach the camp. It's a lot like Hawthorne, but with more tents than barracks. Your main job is the same. You build and take care of roads, build fences, and help fight soil erosion. But when a fire breaks out in the Apache National Forest, you'll be called to help fight it. Preventing fires is also a big job. Ralph Porter, the local fire ranger, has some of you build a new lookout tower. Men in the tower scan the forest, looking for the first signs of smoke.

Porter asks for volunteers for the fire team. They'll be the first ones sent out when a fire is spotted.

"I can make anyone help fight a fire, if I need to," the ranger says. "But I'd rather have volunteers. I won't kid you. It's hard work. And it can be dangerous."

Everyone loaded into the truck when a fire was spotted.

→ To join the fire team, turn to page **96**.

→ To keep building roads, turn to page **98**.

That night the lights go out at 10:00, just as Sergeant Willis said they would. The men in your barracks slowly settle down and fall asleep. You close your eyes. If Joey doesn't come to get you, maybe you'll just stay after all.

"Psst!" The noise startles you. You open your eyes and see Joey.

"Hey," he whispers. "You coming?"

"Um, sure," you whisper back. He leads you out of the barracks and across the training camp. "I checked out the camp after dinner," he says. "There's a hole in the fence around the other side. Come on."

You follow Joey through the darkness. Outside the camp, lights still glow in some of the skyscrapers downtown. Then you slip through the fence.

"That's it," Joey says. "We're free to go."

You tell Joey good-bye and walk to the subway. The CCC just wasn't for you. But you still need a job. You wonder what you're going to tell your mother when you get home.

THE END

To follow another path, turn to page 11.
To read the conclusion, turn to page 101.

They show movies in the recreation hall every other week. You pay your dime to enter and take a seat.

Before the film a newsreel shows news from around the world. Germany's leader, Adolf Hitler, and the Nazi political party are causing lots of trouble. They blame Jewish people for Germany's problems. They are sending many Jews to prison camps.

"I hate those Nazis," Dan says. "Soon they'll get us into another world war."

All through the movie, you think about the sad fate of the Jewish people in Europe. When the movie is over, you talk to one of the army officers in the hall.

"Do you think there's going to be a war in Europe?" you ask.

The officer nods. "I don't see any other way this will end. And if the world goes to war, the United States will be in it."

"Hey Dan," you whisper after lights out. "What do you think about joining the army once we're done here? If there's a war coming, I want to help fight it."

"Are you serious?" he asks. "What will your mother say?"

You know your mom will be upset. But you'll get paid and can keep sending her money. And you've never felt this strongly about anything.

"I'll tell her after I enlist," you say. You're excited for your future now—a future the CCC helped you figure out.

THE END

To follow another path, turn to page 11.
To read the conclusion, turn to page 101.

You, Dan, and some other guys pile into the back of the army truck. It takes you to Oneonta, the town nearest the camp.

Groups of girls are gathered inside the dance hall. Dan nudges you toward two standing near the dance floor.

Dan introduces you, and the girls say their names are Mary and Ellen. You ask Ellen to dance. When the night is over, Ellen smiles.

"I hope you'll be in town for the next dance," she says.

"Sure," you say. "And sometimes we have a big dance out at the lake. Maybe you'd like to go as my date?"

Ellen nods as she takes a pencil and some paper out of her purse. "We don't have a phone at home, just the one at my father's grocery store. But maybe you can write to me."

As the weeks go by, you write to Ellen nearly every day, and she writes back. You see each other whenever you can and even meet her family. One day you receive a letter containing some great news.

"Listen to this," you tell Dan. "The guy who helps Ellen's father at his store is joining the navy. Ellen asked if he would hire me when I'm finished here!"

You read on. The job pays enough that you can still send money to your mother.

Turn the page.

"So the city boy is going to stay in the country," Dan says.

You nod. With a job and a girlfriend, you won't miss the city at all.

CCC enrollees had time for fun as well as for work.

THE END

To follow another path, turn to page 11.
To read the conclusion, turn to page 101.

Frank stays back, but you walk up to the snake. You get down on your knees and peer at it.

"What does it look like?" Frank asks. You describe its tan skin and the darker brown spots on it. You add, "And on the end of its body is something that's making some noise."

Frank starts to back up. "You better get out of there—that's a rattlesnake!"

You stand and start to back away. Your heel hits a rock, and you tumble to the ground, landing next to the snake. You feel a sharp pain in your left hand. Is it from the fall, or did the snake bite? Bert runs over as the snake slithers away.

"Let me see your hand," he says. "Do you feel pain there? Or any tingling in your face?"

Turn the page.

You shake your head.

"Those are some of the signs that a rattler's poison got into you. Even if he bit you, he might not have released any poison."

Bert has you keep your left hand below your heart. "Not many people die from rattlesnake bites, but we had better get you to a doctor just the same."

In Hawthorne the town doctor gives you a shot of antivenin to counteract the snake's venom. He tells you to take it easy the rest of the day. You decide to steer clear of snakes and other wildlife from now on.

THE END

To follow another path, turn to page 11.
To read the conclusion, turn to page 101.

You run to get Bert as Frank moves closer to the snake. "What does it look like?" Bert shouts to Frank as you run back to the pond.

Frank describes the snake's tan skin with darker brown spots. "And on the end of its body is something that's making some noise."

Bert rushes over and pulls Frank back. "You idiot! That's a rattlesnake!"

"We're from the city," you say. "What do we know?"

Bert tells you to never go near any snakes. "Just step back and try not to scare them," he says.

A rattlesnake—you could have been killed! From now on, you'll stick to your work. No more nature walks for you.

THE END

To follow another path, turn to page 11.
To read the conclusion, turn to page 101.

Jose and you both join the fire team. You learn how to cut down a line of trees so the fire won't have enough fuel to spread. Digging trenches is another way to stop the fire.

A few days later, you get your first fire call. You, Jose, and the others jump into a truck. Dark smoke is rising over the forest. As you jump out of the truck, you feel the heat of the flames.

"Head for that line of trees," a foreman yells. "Start cutting them down."

You and Jose swing your axes as fast as you can. Around you, other guys wear water pumps on their backs. They spray water onto the flames.

Night comes, and you find a place to sleep on the ground, away from the flames. When dawn breaks the work starts all over again. As the day goes on, it begins to rain. Between the rain and your hard work, the flames finally die out.

Firefighting is hard, but you like the excitement and the feeling of making a difference. You decide to apply for a job as a New York City firefighter when the Depression is over.

Enrollees cleared grass and trees to form a fire lane blocking the fire.

THE END

To follow another path, turn to page 11.
To read the conclusion, turn to page 101.

Even though you're not on the fire team, you play a role in firefighting. Your team builds roads across the forest, so fire crews can reach fires at their source. You also help build a lookout tower. One day your foreman, Pete, calls you all together.

"There's a big fire on the other side of the mountain. Everybody in camp has to go. Grab a shovel and jump on a truck."

The truck bumps along one of the fire roads until it ends. You and the others jump out of the truck and run toward the fire.

The fire races through the forest. The treetops explode into flames from the heat.

"Start digging!" Pete shouts.

The fire feels like a wall of heat. You gasp from the choking black smoke.

"Nine guys died fighting a fire in Wyoming not too long ago," someone says. "The wind shifted, and they were goners."

Could that happen here? As you dig, Pete calls to you.

"Take the truck down to the nearest tower. Go up and call for more help."

You run back to the truck and head down the road. The fire is still spreading, and you crane your neck to look at it behind you.

BAM! Your head slams into the steering wheel. You glimpse the trunk of the tree you hit, and then everything goes black. You bleed to death alone in the truck, never regaining consciousness.

THE END

To follow another path, turn to page 11.
To read the conclusion, turn to page 101.

As men left to fight World War II, women got jobs in places such as factories and rail yards.

CHAPTER 5

BACK TO PROSPERITY

Despite President Franklin Roosevelt's New Deal, the Great Depression dragged on. The government programs helped the U.S. economy slowly regain strength. But through most of the 1930s, unemployment rates remained much higher than usual.

It took the start of World War II in 1939 to finally put Americans back to work. The U.S. government provided weapons and supplies to several European countries. After the United States entered the war in 1941, U.S. companies produced weapons and supplies for 16 million American troops. People who had struggled to find jobs now had plenty to choose from.

Even before the war, the Bonus Marchers had more money in their pockets. In 1936 Congress voted to give the veterans their bonus. The average amount the vets received was just under $600, and the highest amount was $1,585.

Some members of the Civilian Conservation Corps entered the military even before the war began. The skills and discipline they learned in the corps often helped them advance. The CCC had an impressive record of success. Its 3 million members planted about 3 billion trees, built nearly 50,000 bridges, and developed about 8,000 state parks.

Many of the young people who rode the rails also entered the military. Some say the years they spent searching for food and living in hobo jungles made them tough. That toughness helped them face harsh conditions during the war.

Many CCC enrollees gained job skills that helped them later.

Not all Americans liked Roosevelt and his New Deal. They opposed programs that limited what banks and other companies could do. Others disliked the huge debt the government created as it spent more money than it took in. But the New Deal programs showed Americans that the government could use its power to increase equality and limit suffering.

Some programs, like the WPA and the CCC, disappeared after the Great Depression ended. But many are still in place. Social Security provides money for people who are retired or who have health problems that prevent them from working. The Federal Deposit Insurance Corporation guarantees bank accounts up to $250,000, so people don't lose their savings if their bank fails.

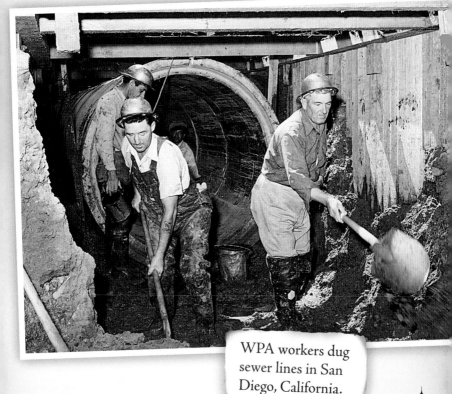

WPA workers dug sewer lines in San Diego, California.

The U.S. economy still struggles at times, such as during the "Great Recession" of 2008–2009. But the odds of another Great Depression are small, thanks to the lessons learned during the 1930s.

Timeline

1929—The stock market crashes on October 29, marking the start of the Great Depression.

1931—A drought begins in the Midwest, creating the Dust Bowl.

1932—In May veterans from across the United States come to Washington, D.C., seeking bonus money.

In July U.S. Army troops attack the Bonus Marchers at their camps.

In November Democrat Franklin Roosevelt defeats Republican President Herbert Hoover, promising Americans a "new deal" to end the Great Depression.

1933—The Civilian Conservation Corps is one of the first of Roosevelt's New Deal programs, putting young men to work in the nation's forests and parks.

Congress creates the Federal Deposit Insurance Corporation.

1935—Congress approves funding for the Works Progress Administration to provide jobs to unemployed Americans.

President Roosevelt signs the Social Security Act.

1936—Congress votes to give the Bonus Marchers their money.

Roosevelt is re-elected president.

1939—World War II begins in Europe, and Roosevelt begins helping Great Britain. Producing this aid helps create jobs in the United States. The United States and other countries begin emerging from the Great Depression.

Autumn rains end the drought in the Dust Bowl.

1941—In December the United States enters World War II. American factories are soon working nonstop to produce weapons and supplies for the military.

OTHER PATHS TO EXPLORE

In this book you've seen how the events experienced during the Great Depression look different from three points of view.

Perspectives on history are as varied as the people who lived it. You can explore other paths on your own to learn more about what happened. Seeing history from many points of view is an important part of understanding it.

Here are some ideas for other Great Depression points of view to explore:

+ During the Depression teachers were paid very little or sometimes nothing at all. What would it have been like to try to teach school during that time?

+ The National Labor Relations Act of 1935 gave workers the right to join labor unions. What would it have been like to organize or belong to a labor union at a time when competition was high for jobs?

+ Not everyone was poor during the Depression. What would it have been like to be a member of a wealthy family during a time when so many were without basic necessities?

READ MORE

Bolden, Tonya. *FDR's Alphabet Soup: New Deal America, 1932–1937.* New York: Alfred A. Knopf, 2010.

Elish, Dan. *Franklin Delano Roosevelt.* New York: Marshall Cavendish Benchmark, 2009.

Lassier, Allison. *The Dust Bowl: An Interactive History Adventure.* Mankato, Minn.: Capstone Press, 2009.

Nardo, Don. *The Great Depression.* Detroit: Lucent Books, 2008.

INTERNET SITES

FactHound offers a safe, fun way to find Internet sites related to this book. All of the sites on FactHound have been researched by our staff.

Here's all you do:
Visit *www.facthound.com*
Type in this code: 9781429654807

GLOSSARY

barracks (BEAR-uhks)—buildings often used to house soldiers

Communism (KAHM-yuh-ni-zuhm)—a way of organizing a country so that all property belongs to the government, and the profits are shared by all

erosion (i-ROH-zhuhn)—the wearing away of soil by water or wind

interest (IN-tur-ist)—a fee paid for borrowing money

Jewish (JOO-ish)—describing Judaism, a religion based on a belief in one God and the teachings of a holy book called the Torah

Nazi (NOT-zee)—a member of Adolf Hitler's National Socialist German Workers' Party

110

racism (RAY-siz-uhm)—a belief that one race is better than another race

recruit (ri-KROOT)—a person who has just joined a group or organization

shanty (SHAN-tee)—a small, poorly built home

veteran (VET-ur-uhn)—a person who has served in the military

BIBLIOGRAPHY

Davis, Kenneth S. *FDR: The New Deal Years, 1933–1937.* New York: Random House, 1986.

Dickson, Paul, and Thomas B. Allen. *The Bonus Army: An American Epic.* New York: Walker & Company, 2004.

Dickstein, Morris. *Dancing in the Dark: A Cultural History of the Great Depression.* New York: W. W. Norton, 2009.

Kolvet, Renee Corona, and Victoria Ford. *The Civilian Conservation Corps in Nevada: From Boys to Men.* Reno: University of Nevada Press, 2006.

Kyvig, David E. *Daily Life in the United States, 1920–1940.* Chicago: Ivan R. Dee, 2004.

McElvaine, Robert S., ed. *Down & Out in the Great Depression: Letters from the Forgotten Man.* Chapel Hill: University of North Carolina Press, 1983.

Purvis, Louis Lester. *The Ace in the Hole: A Brief History of Company 818 of the Civilian Conservation Corps.* Columbus, Ga.: Brentwood Christian Press, 1989.

Sommer, Barbara W. *Hard Work and a Good Deal: The Civilian Conservation Corps in Minnesota.* St. Paul: Minnesota Historical Society Press, 2008.

Uys, Errol Lincoln. *Riding the Rails: Teenagers on the Move During the Great Depression.* New York: TV Books, 2000.

INDEX